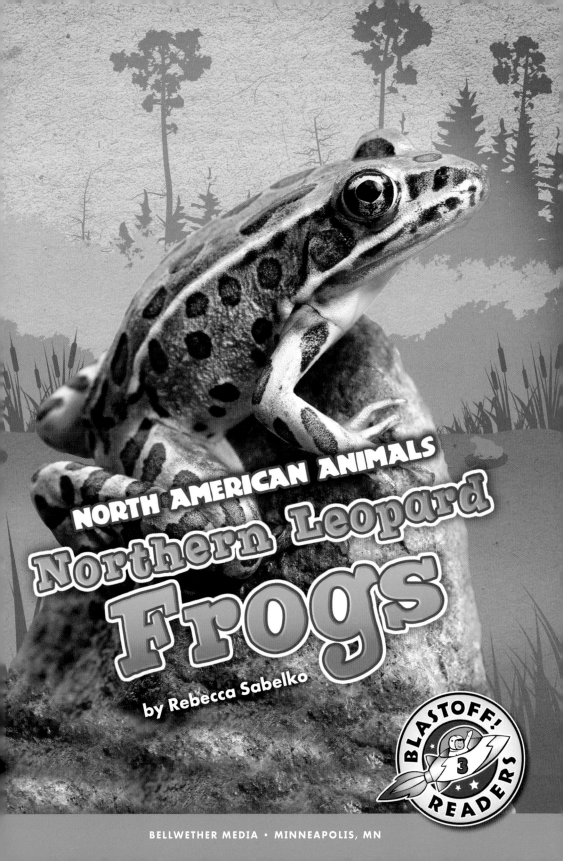

NORTH AMERICAN ANIMALS

Northern Leopard Frogs

by Rebecca Sabelko

BLASTOFF!
3
READERS

BELLWETHER MEDIA • MINNEAPOLIS, MN

Note to Librarians, Teachers, and Parents:

Blastoff! Readers are carefully developed by literacy experts and combine standards-based content with developmentally appropriate text.

Level 1 provides the most support through repetition of high-frequency words, light text, predictable sentence patterns, and strong visual support.

Level 2 offers early readers a bit more challenge through varied simple sentences, increased text load, and less repetition of high-frequency words.

Level 3 advances early-fluent readers toward fluency through increased text and concept load, less reliance on visuals, longer sentences, and more literary language.

Level 4 builds reading stamina by providing more text per page, increased use of punctuation, greater variation in sentence patterns, and increasingly challenging vocabulary.

Level 5 encourages children to move from "learning to read" to "reading to learn" by providing even more text, varied writing styles, and less familiar topics.

Whichever book is right for your reader, Blastoff! Readers are the perfect books to build confidence and encourage a love of reading that will last a lifetime!

This edition first published in 2019 by Bellwether Media, Inc.

No part of this publication may be reproduced in whole or in part without written permission of the publisher. For information regarding permission, write to Bellwether Media, Inc., Attention: Permissions Department, 6012 Blue Circle Drive, Minnetonka, MN 55343.

Library of Congress Cataloging-in-Publication Data

Names: Sabelko, Rebecca, author.
Title: Northern Leopard Frogs / by Rebecca Sabelko.
Description: Minneapolis, MN : Bellwether Media, Inc., 2019. | Series:
  Blastoff! Readers. North American Animals | Audience: Age 5-8. | Audience:
  K to Grade 3. | Includes bibliographical references and index.
Identifiers: LCCN 2018030418 (print) | LCCN 2018032518 (ebook) | ISBN
  9781681036441 (ebook) | ISBN 9781626179134 (hardcover : alk. paper)
Subjects: LCSH: Northern leopard frog–Juvenile literature.
Classification: LCC QL668.E27 (ebook) | LCC QL668.E27 S23 2019 (print) | DDC 597.8/9-dc23
LC record available at https://lccn.loc.gov/2018030418

Editor: Kate Moening   Designer: Josh Brink

Printed in the United States of America, North Mankato, MN.

Table of Contents

What Are Northern Leopard Frogs?

Northern leopard frogs are **amphibians** that live in ponds and **meadows**. They are often called meadow frogs.

northern leopard frog range =

conservation status: least concern

Extinct

Extinct in the Wild

Critically Endangered

Endangered

Vulnerable

Near Threatened

Least Concern

They live in the northeastern and central United States. They are also found in parts of the western U.S. and southern Canada.

Northern leopard frogs have
dark brown spots on their backs
and legs. These spots may
have a white or yellow border.

Identify a Northern Leopard Frog

white belly

dark brown spots

raised lines along back

Raised lines run down their backs. But their bellies are smooth and white.

Northern leopard frogs
are usually 2 to 5 inches
(5 to 13 centimeters) long.

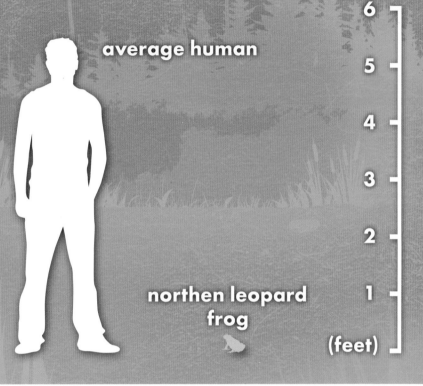

Size of a Northern Leopard Frog

average human

northen leopard frog

6

5

4

3

2

1

(feet)

Like many amphibians, female northern leopard frogs are larger than males.

Hopping Homes

Northern leopard frogs **hibernate** each winter beneath frozen ponds or lakes. They meet each spring in calm, warm water to **breed**.

Then, they **migrate** to meadows for the summer. They get water by **absorbing** dew through their skin!

dew

Northern leopard frogs try to **confuse** their enemies. They hop in a **zigzag** when they are chased. This makes them hard to catch.

Some northern leopard frogs look like poisonous pickerel frogs. This tricks **predators** into thinking they are poisonous, too!

pickerel frog

13

American bullfrogs

raccoons

great blue herons

red-tailed hawks

Sometimes, northern leopard frogs cannot escape. They scream when they are caught.

This surprises their predators!
They spit the frogs out.
Then, the frogs hop to safety!

Northern leopard frogs are not picky eaters. They eat any animals they can fit into their mouths!

common garter snakes

chorus frogs

earthworms

wolf spiders

field crickets

house flies

These **carnivores** wait for **prey** to pass close by. They use their strong legs to spring toward their meal.

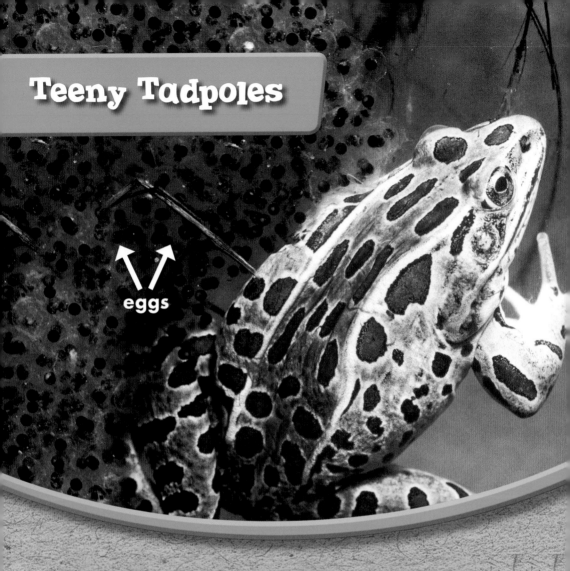

Teeny Tadpoles

eggs

Northern leopard frogs begin to breed in March. Females lay groups of eggs that stick to water plants. The egg groups are 2 to 6 inches (5 to 15 centimeters) wide.

Baby Facts

Name for babies:	tadpoles
Number of eggs laid:	up to 7,000 eggs
Time spent inside egg:	1 to 3 weeks
Time spent with mom:	1 day

tadpole

The eggs **hatch** in one to three weeks. Small **tadpoles** explore their pond and begin to grow.

The tadpoles grow legs and lose their tails over a few months. Then, they hop to find a meadow to call home!

Glossary

absorbing—taking in

amphibians—animals that are able to live both on land and in water

breed—to produce offspring

carnivores—animals that only eat meat

confuse—to make something difficult to understand

hatch—to break out of an egg

hibernate—to spend the winter sleeping or resting

meadows—fields of grass

migrate—to travel from one place to another, often with the seasons

predators—animals that hunt other animals for food

prey—animals that are hunted by other animals for food

tadpoles—baby northern leopard frogs

zigzag—a path that has short, sharp turns

To Learn More

AT THE LIBRARY

Howell, Izzi. *Amphibians*. New York, N.Y.:
Rosen Publishing, 2017.

Mahoney, Emily. *20 Fun Facts About Amphibian
Adaptations*. New York, N.Y.: Gareth Stevens
Publishing, 2017.

Mattern, Joanne. *Frogs and Toads*. Egremont, Mass.:
Red Chair Press, 2017.

ON THE WEB

FACTSURFER

Factsurfer.com gives you
a safe, fun way to find
more information.

1. Go to www.factsurfer.com.

2. Enter "northern leopard frogs"
   into the search box.

3. Click the "Surf" button and select your
   book cover to see a list of related web sites.

Index

The images in this book are reproduced through the courtesy of: Alexander Sviridov, front cover, pp. 4-5; Skip Moody/ Dembinsky Photo Associates/ Alamy p. 6; Hailshadow, pp. 7 (top left), 8; Paul Reeves Photography, p. 7 (middle, right); Michiel de Wit, pp. 7 (bottom), 9, 17 (top left); Chris Hill, p. 10; Dan Ross, p. 11; Stephen Dalton/ Newscom, p. 12; Matt Jeppson, p. 13; JIANG HONGYAN, p. 14 (top left); Eric Isselee, p. 14 (top right); Tathoms, p. 14 (bottom left); Le Do, p. 14 (bottom right); Jason Patrick Ross, p. 15; Tom Worsley, p. 16; Nashepard, p. 17 (top right); yevgeniy11, p. 17 (middle left); Cristina Romero Palma, p. 17 (middle right); PetlinDmitry, p. 17 (bottom left); irin-k, p. 17 (bottom right); Gary Meszaros/ Getty Images, p. 18; ZUMA Press/ Alamy, p. 19; John Mitchell/ Getty Images, p. 20; BHamms, p. 21.